For

⸭⸭

From

⸭⸭

Date

⸭⸭

© 2012 by Barbour Publishing, Inc.

Compiled and written by Janice Hanna.

ISBN 978-1-61626-413-0

Scripture quotations marked KJV are taken from the King James Version of the Bible.

Scripture quotations marked NIV are taken from the HOLY BIBLE, NEW INTERNATIONAL VERSION®. NIV®. Copyright © 1973, 1978, 1984, 2011 by Biblica, Inc.™ Used by permission. All rights reserved worldwide.

Scripture quotations marked NASB are taken from the New American Standard Bible, © 1960, 1962, 1963, 1968, 1971, 1972, 1973, 1975, 1977, 1995 by The Lockman Foundation. Used by permission.

Scripture quotations marked MSG are from *THE MESSAGE*. Copyright © by Eugene H. Peterson 1993, 1994, 1995, 1996, 2000, 2001, 2002. Used by permission of NavPress Publishing Group.

Published by Barbour Publishing, Inc., P.O. Box 719, Uhrichsville, Ohio 44683, www.barbourbooks.com

Our mission is to publish and distribute inspirational products offering exceptional value and biblical encouragement to the masses.

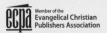

Member of the
Evangelical Christian
Publishers Association

Printed in China.

Today,

GOD

Wants You to Know...

365 Pieces of Heavenly Wisdom

DAY 1

You are loved.

◆

Think of it: unconditional love!
Before God created you, He loved you.
After He created you, He continues
to love you, no matter what.
He has placed love in your life
that you can give and receive—
family, friends, coworkers, neighbors.
Love because you are loved today.

DAY 2

God has great plans for your life!

Today might seem like a dead end, but God promises He's got it under control—today, tomorrow, and forever. "I know what I'm doing. I have it all planned out—plans to take care of you, not abandon you, plans to give you the future you hope for" (Jeremiah 29:11 MSG).

DAY 3

You don't have to deal with your struggles alone.

◆

We look at our burdens and heavy loads and shrink from them; but as we lift them and bind them with our hearts, they become wings; and on them we rise and soar toward God.

Mrs. Charles E. Cowman

DAY 4

You are not ruled by your personality.

◆

Have you ever blamed something on your personality—maybe an outburst of temper or a tendency toward laziness? It's time to stop playing the blame game. We were all created with unique personalities, but they do not define us.

DAY 5

Chains can be broken in your life.

◆

Sometimes it feels like we're stuck, bound up by the chains of the past. There's good news today! God is in the chain-breaking business. Ask Him to set you free from the things that have held you bound, then watch as those chains are broken.

DAY 6

You have great hope.

◆

Imagine a burglar broke into your
home and stole your television,
or perhaps your computer.
You would feel violated of course.
Many things can be stolen from us,
but no one can take away our hope.
We can cling fast to it, even when
everything else crumbles.

DAY 7

You can toss your cares overboard.

◆

Ever feel like your cares are weighing
you down? Like they are an anchor?
Today, God wants you to know
that you can toss those anchors
overboard! Get rid of them.
See them sinking to the bottom
of the sea of forgetfulness.

DAY 8

You can have an impact on your world.

◆

Did you know that you can make a difference in the lives around you? It's true! With a kind word or a smile, you can impact your world for the better. Today, step out of your comfort zone. Make an impact.

DAY 9

You are fearfully and wonderfully made.

◆

Ever dislike what you see in the mirror? Find yourself being critical of your appearance? God didn't make a mistake when He picked out your nose, your hair color, or your physique. He knew just what He was doing, in fact. So, instead of struggling with your looks. . .celebrate them! You are fearfully and wonderfully made.

DAY 10

You are worth the investment.

◆

Do you ever wonder about your value?
No need! You are the most valuable
thing in the world to God, and you are
worth His investment.

DAY 11

Rough relationships really can get better.

◆

Struggling through a tough
relationship? Ready to give up? Don't!
Rough relationships can be mended.
Consider using these twelve words,
which could heal any relationship:
I love you. I was wrong. I'm sorry.
Please forgive me.

DAY 12

Sometimes being idle is a good thing.

◆

As Henry Wadsworth Longfellow once said, to "Sit in reverie and watch the changing color of the waves that break upon the idle seashore of the mind" can be a lovely thing. Today, spend a little time resting and relaxing.

DAY 13

A bad hair day doesn't have to mean a bad day.

◆

Ever had a really bad hair day. . . a day when nothing seemed to be going right? Even on the toughest day, you can still keep a cheerful countenance. Folks will be so intrigued by your happy expression that they won't even notice your hair.

DAY 14

There is a peace that passes understanding.

◆

If you've ever walked through a really rough season, you know how it can affect your nerves. Today, God wants you to know that He can give you a peace that passes understanding, even when you're going through a rough spell. Lean on Him. Breathe deeply. Feel His peace.

DAY 15

Only believe.

◆

I believe in the sun, even when it is
not shining. I believe in love,
even when I do not feel it. I believe
in God, even when He is silent.

UNKNOWN

DAY 16

God really is interested in what you're going through.

◆

Ever feel like no one's paying attention? Like you're going through life completely unnoticed? There is One who is paying close attention, and He's genuinely interested in what you're going through today. Spend time with Him. Listen to His words of love spoken over you.

DAY 17

Prayer is the main work.

◆

Many of us work from sunup till sundown. We slave away, motivated and driven. However, we often overlook the one "work" that really makes a difference: prayer. Today, make a decision to pray like you've never prayed before.

DAY 18

You really can whistle while you work.

◆

Remember the song that the seven dwarves sang? They whistled while they worked, and it eased the workload. The song might have originated in a fairy tale, but the concept is very true. You really can enjoy your work by adding a little tune.

DAY 19

There are no tears in heaven.

◆

Life is filled with heartbreaking moments. Isn't it consoling to know that there will be no tears in heaven? No pain. No heartbreak. No anguish. Heaven will be a place of joy and celebration. What a glorious place that will be!

DAY 20

Humor softens life's blows.

◆

Through humor, you can soften some of the worst blows that life delivers. And once you find laughter, no matter how painful your situation might be, you can survive it.

BILL COSBY

DAY 21

God is with you wherever you go.

◆

Ever feel like you've wandered too far? Like God can't find you? Today, He wants you to know that He's with you, no matter where you go. If you climb to the top of a mountain, He's there. If you're in a low place, He's right there beside you.

DAY 22

Being a first-rate version of yourself is better than being a second-rate version of someone else.

◆

How many times do we try to fit in. . . to be like others? Being yourself—even if you're unique, quirky, or offbeat—is always best. Instead of trying to be like someone in your peer group, strive to be the very best you that you can be.

DAY 23

You are needed and wanted.

We all go through seasons in our lives
where we feel left out or unwanted.
Here's good news: You are always
needed and wanted by the Lord.
He will never leave you or forsake you,
and He loves you with an eternal love.

DAY 24

God won't let you down.

◆

Ever been disappointed by someone
you thought you could trust? You're
certainly not alone. Today, God wants
you to know that you can trust Him.
He won't let you down. . .ever. So,
take a deep breath. You can rest easy,
knowing He's on your side.

DAY 25

A crisis isn't a crisis to God.

◆

When we go through an earth-shaking time, we're usually caught off-guard. God isn't shaken though. He knew this was coming and has a plan to see you through. Trust Him in the middle of the crisis. Don't let go.

DAY 26

It's okay to be at a loss for words.

◆

God understands our prayers
even when we can't find
the words to say them.

UNKNOWN

DAY 27

He loves to surprise His kids.

◆

God is in the surprising business.
Just about the time you think you've
got Him figured out. . .surprise!
He startles you with an unexpected
heavenly touch, just what you need
at just the right time!

DAY 28

All achievements begin as an idea.

◆

Did you ever think about the fact
that your ideas and plans come from
above? Many are divinely inspired.
Today, God wants to encourage you to
act on those God-given ideas. Watch
as those ideas morph into reality.

DAY 29

God is near.

It might seem like God is far away,
but He's not. He's closer than your
closest friend, and will stick with you
when others fail you.

DAY 30

You've already made a lot of progress.

◆

Ever feel like giving up? Like the journey is just too hard? Instead of focusing on the road ahead, take a quick glance back. Look how far you've come! Once you see the distance you've already traveled, the road ahead won't look so daunting.

DAY 31

Don't get all shook up!

◆

Man's extremity is God's opportunity.
Unshakable faith is faith that has
been shaken.

UNKNOWN

DAY 32

Where He guides, He provides.

◆

God wouldn't lead you somewhere, only to leave you barren and destitute in that place. He has a plan for your success and is guiding you, even now. Just listen, then follow.

DAY 33

Life is so much more than what your eyes can see.

◆

Ever wish you had bionic vision? That you could see beyond today's circumstances? God is working in amazing ways. Oh, if only you could catch a glimpse of what's going on in the heavenlies right now!

DAY 34

Getting your way is not always for the best.

◆

Are you accustomed to getting your own way? Do you struggle with a "me first" mentality? If so, it's time to let that go. Putting others first is God's way. Sure, it's not always easy, but it's always right.

DAY 35

What really matters is what happens in us, not to us.

◆

Most of us go through rough seasons in our lives, seasons when unfair things happen. Sometimes we let those seasons define us. It's time to change the way we see ourselves. What happens in us is far more important than what happens to us.
What's happening in you today?

DAY 36

Joy is contagious.

Have you ever been in a room where someone started laughing? Before long, the next person was laughing. . . and then the next. Just about the time you thought you could contain your giggles, out they came! Don't fight it. Let the joy flow!

DAY 37

You can triumph over hardship.

◆

Many people go through hardships
and never recover. They end up
coiled up in a ball, tightly wound
(and bound) by the pain. Hardship
doesn't have to end this way.
You were created to triumph,
even over the toughest things.
Today, begin to see yourself as a victor.

DAY 38

When you bless others, you've blessed the Lord.

◆

Did you know that giving a cup of cold water to a stranger is like giving water to God Himself? It's true! "The King will reply, 'Truly I tell you, whatever you did for one of the least of these brothers and sisters of mine, you did for me'" (Matthew 25:40 NIV).

DAY 39

Sometimes we have to go to places we don't want to go.

◆

Ever had that "I don't want to go there" attitude? We're often called to go places—physically, emotionally, spiritually—that we don't want to go. Only on the other side of the journey do we realize the significance. Don't be afraid. Go.

DAY 40

You can persevere.

◆

Patience and perseverance have
a magical effect before which
difficulties disappear and obstacles
vanish. A little knowledge that acts
is worth infinitely more than much
knowledge that is idle.

JOHN QUINCY ADAMS

DAY 41

It might be time for an "I" exam.

◆

Today, God wants you to spend the day noticing how many times you start a sentence with the words "I," "me," and "my." Perhaps it's time to shift your focus.

DAY 42

There is rest for the weary.

◆

Do you ever feel so exhausted that you can't sleep? If so, you're not alone. People all over the globe have worked themselves into a sleepless frenzy. Thank goodness, there is a rest for the weary. . .and it's a deep-rooted rest, one found only in the Lord.

DAY 43

Life really does have a backspace key.

◆

Oy, those mistakes! We make so many
of them! If you're like most people,
you want to slink away and hide
after messing up. Thank goodness,
life really does have a backspace key.
When you ask the Lord to forgive the
mess-ups of the past, He erases them.
They're gone. . .forever!

DAY 44

Life is more than existing.

◆

Ever feel like you're just existing?
Just holding on? Today, God
wants you to know that you can
have abundant life—life that is
adventurous, exciting, and filled with
new destinations. There's so much
more out there for you. Why just exist
when you can really live?

DAY 45

It's not about the money.

◆

Many people make the mistake
of thinking that all the challenges
in their lives would dissipate if they
just had enough money. Nothing
could be further from the truth.
Earning more money, in and of itself,
rarely frees people.

ANTHONY ROBBINS

DAY 46

He wants to clean out your closets.

◆

Ever spent a day clearing out your closet? Likely you ditched the clothes and shoes that didn't fit, then spent some time re-organizing. There are times when we need to take inventory of our "soul closets." We allow condemning thoughts or bitterness to take root in our soul. Time to clean that mess up!

DAY 47

Halfway between yesterday and tomorrow you can find peace.

◆

When you're worried about tomorrow, it's hard to be peaceful. And when you refuse to let go of the pain of yesterday, true, lasting peace never comes. The very best place to find peace—real, lasting peace— is by living in today.

DAY 48

A clear conscience makes a soft pillow.

◆

Guilt can keep us awake nights,
no doubt about it. Today, if you're
struggling with guilt, ask the Lord to
forgive you for what you've done, then
hand it to Him. Once you've dealt
with it, you'll sleep like a baby.

DAY 49

Your life is a movie that others are watching.

◆

And now, starring in the role of a lifetime. . .you! Yes, you! Your life is really a movie that others—friends, family members, church members, teachers, children, and so forth— are watching. What sort of performance are you giving them? One that will take home the prize?

DAY 50

You can reach great heights.

◆

The heights by great men reached
and kept were not obtained by
sudden flight. But they, while their
companions slept, were toiling
upward in the night.

THOMAS S. MONSON

DAY 51

The gifts inside of you are meant to be shared.

◆

Imagine you had a wonderful Christmas gift for a friend. You gave it to her and watched as she took a peek inside, then laid it aside. Surely that's how God feels when we don't utilize the gifts He's given us. Take those gifts out! Show them off. Use them to share joy with everyone you meet.

DAY 52

There are pages of your life not yet written.

◆

Sometimes it's fun to think of your life as a novel that's only practically written. What chapter are you on? How many chapters are behind you? How many are in front of you? Today, the Lord wants you to know that the upcoming chapters in your life's story are going to be filled with His goodness and mercy.

DAY 53

Your transformation will change others.

◆

Perhaps you've heard the old expression: "Changed lives change lives." It's so true. When you've been through a transformation—physical, emotional, spiritual, or otherwise— you want to shout it from the rooftops, and others are sure to respond.

DAY 54

Ask and it will be given to you.

◆

There's an interesting verse in the Bible that says, "You do not have because you do not ask" (James 4:2 NIV). If you're lacking something, take the time to ask.

DAY 55

If you aim above the mark, you'll come closer to hitting it.

◆

Ever have that "just getting by" mentality? You swing low, then wonder why you don't hit the mark? Today, go out of your way to aim high. You might just be surprised at what you hit!

DAY 56

Opportunities are often disguised.

◆

We are all faced with a series of great opportunities brilliantly disguised as impossible situations.

CHARLES R. SWINDOLL

DAY 57

You discover who you are through life's challenges.

◆

Want to find out who you really are? Want to know if you've got the goods? Try going through a few challenges. There's nothing like a little time in the fire to find out if you can survive the purification process.

DAY 58

You have God-given gifts and abilities.

◆

Did you know that your talents come from God? Sure, you can practice at the piano, but He gave you the desire to play in the first place. Sure, you can practice those ballet moves, but He put the desire to dance inside of you!

DAY 59

You don't have to believe the lies that have been spoken to you.

◆

Perhaps you've been lied to. You've been told dozens—or even hundreds—of things about yourself that simply aren't true. Maybe you've believed those lies, not knowing the difference. Today, the Lord wants you to know that a lie is a lie. Don't believe it! Break its hold over you!

DAY 60

God is pleased to call you His child.

◆

Parents know the joy of saying,
"This is my little girl!" or "This is my
little boy." We're so proud to claim our
children. (Until they get to their teens,
anyway!) Doesn't it make you smile to
know that God is pleased to say,
"This one is mine! I adore him/her!"

DAY 61

Learn to laugh
at yourself.

Laughing at our mistakes can lengthen
our own life. Laughing at someone
else's can shorten it.

CULLEN HIGHTOWER

DAY 62

Sometimes it costs more to do nothing than to do something.

◆

Have you ever considered the fact that apathy is expensive? It's true. Doing nothing can be very costly— to your relationships, your career, even your emotional and spiritual state. The next time you feel the nudge to do something. . .get busy!

DAY 63

Patience is the companion of wisdom.

◆

If you've ever met a truly wise person, then you probably notice that he has a higher patience level than most. Patience walks hand-in-hand with wisdom. So, how's your patience level today? Before you claim to be wise, take a second look. Patience, my friend! Patience!

DAY 64

God doesn't look at the outward appearance.

◆

Aren't you glad God doesn't pay attention to your outward appearance? He's not standing nearby to critique your hairstyle, skin color, weight, or height. Instead, His penetrating gaze is directed at something you can't see—your heart.

DAY 65

The battle belongs to the Lord.

◆

If you're facing a formidable foe today, remember, the battle isn't yours to fight. It never was. Suit up in your armor, but trust the Lord to win the battle on your behalf.

DAY 66

There's peace in the middle.

◆

Having spent the better part of my life trying to either relive the past or experience the future before it arrives, I have come to believe that in between these two extremes is peace.

UNKNOWN

DAY 67

No matter where you've come from, you are usable to God.

◆

Maybe you think your background—where you've come from—limits you from being used by God to do mighty things. Nothing could be further from the truth! All of the great men and women of the Bible had a "past." Aren't you glad that God chooses people to impact the world according to His criteria, not ours?

DAY 68

The best way to have the last word is to apologize.

◆

Oh, how we love to have the last word!
We clinch our fists, ready with
a comeback, even before the other
person finishes speaking. Today,
take a deep breath. Consider
apologizing, even if you don't feel at fault.
That way, you'll always have the last word.

DAY 69

God plus one equals a majority.

◆

When you take the time to pray before
making decisions, you can move
forward with the assurance that God
is right there, guiding you all the way.
Even if no one else chooses to go
along for the ride, you are not alone.
And remember, even if you feel alone,
God plus one equals a majority.

DAY 70

He's ready for an instant message. . .right now!

◆

We live in an "instant" world, don't
we? Text messages, instant message,
social networking—everything is so
quick. Today, God wants you to know
that He's standing by, ready for an
"instant" encounter with you.

DAY 71

Freedom of religion comes at great cost.

◆

Likely you've heard the expression: "Freedom isn't free." It comes at great cost to those who risk their lives to protect it. Today, as you contemplate your religious freedom, take the time to pray for those who've made it possible.

DAY 72

Children need to feel cherished.

◆

Children will not remember you
for the material things you provided
but for the feeling that you
cherished them.

RICHARD L. EVANS

DAY 73

You don't need to rely on yourself for energy.

◆

These days, people all over the world feel zapped of energy. They drink energy drinks, hoping to "pep up" their levels. If you want a lasting dose of energy, go to the real supplier—the Lord. He can energize you and give you the zeal to face life's challenges.

DAY 74

Rome wasn't built in a day.

◆

We're always in such a hurry, aren't we? It's hard to remember that not everything happens at once. Some things require time, patience, and great effort. Instead of rushing toward the goal, step back and take a look at the details. Then inch your way forward, building brick by brick.

DAY 75

These are the good old days.

◆

People are always asking about the good old days. I say, why don't you say the good now days?

ROBERT M. YOUNG

DAY 76

God doesn't have an ax to grind with you.

◆

Some people wander away from
the Lord then refuse to come back
because they think He'll be mad at
them. Nothing could be further
from the truth! God has no ax
to grind with you, even if you've
wandered from the fold. He longs for
you to come back home so that He
can sweep you into His arms.

DAY 77

There's a time to stop talking and just listen.

◆

Oh, how we love to get a word
in edgewise, even if it means
interrupting someone to do so.
After all, our opinion is valuable. . .
right? Today, God wants you to know
that listening is a specialized skill.
Not everyone does it well, but He
longs for you to try.

DAY 78

God really cares about your achy-breaky heart.

◆

If you've walked through a
particularly rough relationship or
have experienced a broken heart,
the Lord cares a great deal. He longs
for you to get past the pain and learn
to trust again.

DAY 79

Many hands make light work.

◆

Don't you love working alongside others? There's something so wonderful about joining with friends to get a job done. The task is lighter, the conversation is cheerful, and the result is a job well done.

DAY 80

It's not good for all of our wishes to come true.

◆

It is not good for all our wishes to be
filled; through sickness we recognize
the value of health; through evil,
the value of good; through hunger,
the value of food; through exertion,
the value of rest.

GREEK PROVERB

DAY 81

You are the apple of God's eye.

◆

Likely you've heard the expression: "She's the apple of her father's eye." Even if you didn't have a great relationship with your earthly father, God wants you to know that you're the apple of His eye. His heart swells with joy when He thinks about you.

DAY 82

You are a work in progress.

◆

We get frustrated when we don't see the kind of progress in our lives that we hope for. We want to rush the process. Remember, you are a work in progress! Inch by inch, mile by mile. . . you're growing.

DAY 83

A hug is a great gift!

◆

Doesn't it feel great to have someone
wrap their arms around you and tell
you that everything is going to be
okay? Today, you can be that someone.
Wrap your arms around a friend and
whisper in her ear, "Everything is
going to be fine."

DAY 84

You can crawl up into your Daddy's lap.

◆

If you had a good relationship with
your father when you were a child,
perhaps you remember crawling up
into his lap, leaning your head on his
shoulder, and listening to him tell you
a story. Your Daddy God longs for
you to crawl up in His lap today.
He has much to tell you!

DAY 85

No man is rich enough to buy back his past.

◆

Aren't you glad the past is behind you?
Greater still, it's never coming back.
All of those mistakes of yesterday. . .
they're dead and gone. Even if
you owned every bank in town,
you couldn't buy back your yesterdays.

DAY 86

There are children around the globe who need your love.

◆

Sometimes we get so caught up in the day-to-day grind that we forget the needs of children around the globe. If you've never considered sponsoring a child or supporting a foreign missionary, perhaps today is your day!

DAY 87

God is not a liar.

◆

If you're like most people, you've
been lied to. It hurts, doesn't it? And it
breaks trust. Once that person lies to
you, it's harder to believe him the next
time. Aren't you glad God isn't a liar?
If He said it. . .He'll do it!

DAY 88

Even the most disagreeable people can be won over with a smile.

◆

When you come in contact with a cranky person, how do you respond? Does their crankiness rub off on you? Truth is, even cranky, bitter people respond better to honey than vinegar. You're much more likely to see a sticky situation turned around with a smile than a frown.

DAY 89

The Lord watches over your comings and goings.

◆

We rush out the door to work, then buzz down the road, radio blaring. We stop off at the store, then run by a friend's house before going home at night. All along the way, the Lord has His eye on us. We're never out of His sight. His love for us is so deep that He just can't take His eyes off of us!

DAY 90

You can take action today.

◆

Been feeling stuck? Got your feet
in the mud? Even if your situation
has held you captive, this is your day
to break free. Take action. Make a
move. Don't hold back. Step forward
. . .and watch God work.

DAY 91

Broken hearts can become brand new.

◆

The pain of a broken heart can be devastating. Crushing, even. Isn't it good to know the Lord is in the heart-mending business? He can take that broken heart and breathe new life into it, making it even better than new.

DAY 92

The first will be last and the last will be first.

◆

Some things in life just don't seem fair. Oftentimes people are elevated— at work, in sports, with their artistic gifts—and we feel left behind. Doesn't it make you feel good to know that the first will be last and the last will be first? Even if you've been lagging at the end of the line, your day is coming!

DAY 93

Morning is coming.

◆

We go through seasons where it
feels like someone turned out the
light. Everything is dark. Dreary.
We can't seem to get past the pain
that comes with the night. Today,
God wants you to know that morning
is coming. There will be a bright,
new sunrise, and all of the pain you've
faced in the night will fade away,
like the morning dew.

DAY 94

With God on your side, you really can be bold and courageous.

◆

Are you the timid sort? Afraid to speak your mind? Shiver and shake when you think of standing in front of people? There's good news! The same God who gave David the courage to take down the mighty Goliath stands ready to embolden you with courage, too!

DAY 95

You are called, chosen, and set apart.

◆

Before the foundation of time, God knew your name. He chose you for Himself. Isn't that an amazing thought? Before the planet was formed, God was thinking of you!

DAY 96

God's idea of success might be a little different from yours.

We all have such unique ideas about success. To some, it's a large bank account or a big house. To many, it's landing the perfect job. Today, God wants you to know that His definition of success has nothing to do with those things. He's far more interested in your heart than your fancy car.

DAY 97

The beauty of creation is all around you.

◆

What a perfect day to stop and look
around you. Enjoy the beauty of
creation. The trees. Wide-open fields.
Mountains. Rivers. Streams.
Crisp, fallen leaves. Budding flowers.
How often do we drive right past
these things and never see them?
Creation beckons!

DAY 98

He loves it when you set apart a day to worship Him.

◆

We worship God every day of the week. Some people would say that worshipping alone—apart from others—suits them just fine. But there's something about coming together with other believers that strengthens us and brings great joy to the heart of God.

DAY 99

God can help you at the fork in the road.

◆

Sometimes life presents us with "Eenie-Meenie-Miney-Moe" moments. We stand at a proverbial fork in the road and have no idea which way to turn. We're hesitant to move forward, for fear of making a mistake. Just remember, God is standing right there alongside us, whispering, "Turn this way!"

DAY 100

Common sense is not always common.

◆

Have you ever met someone who's book smart but doesn't seem to have common sense? No matter how many degrees you have, nothing can take the place of good old common sense.

DAY 101

When you trust God, He makes your path straight.

◆

Ever set off on a path, only to find yourself going down a rabbit trail? You accidentally turn off, then find yourself lost? It happens all the time. Thank goodness the Lord has a way of wooing you back to the right road. Listen closely! He's giving you instructions, even now.

DAY 102

You have a Father who will never leave you or forsake you.

◆

If you've ever known the pain of rejection by an earthly father, then perhaps you have a hard time relating to God as a father figure. Today, He wants you to know that—no matter how much rejection you've faced in the past—He will never leave you or forsake you.

DAY 103

Falling off the wagon isn't the end of the road.

◆

We all make mistakes. We all fall.
Sometimes we stumble in private,
where no one sees us. Other times,
we crater in front of a crowd. Even if
you've messed up in a huge (or public)
way, take heart. You can begin again.
Stand up. Brush yourself off.
Keep on keepin' on.

DAY 104

It is possible to renew your mind.

Ever wish you could clear your mind
of all the junk? Need an overhaul
of your thought-life? With God's
help, you really can erase the bad and
replace it with good. Your mind—
and your heart—can be renewed
(just like new). All you have to do is ask.

DAY 105

You can go on learning, no matter your age.

◆

It doesn't matter if you're two or ninety-two, it's never too late to learn. Staying on a learning curve will keep you sharp, alert, and aware of what's going on around you. Today, make up your mind to be a perpetual student.

DAY 106

God is the potter, we are the clay.

◆

Ever try to shape yourself into someone you're not, just to impress people? Today, God wants you to know that He's the one doing the shaping. We're the clay. He's the one with hands extended, molding us into His image.

DAY 107

Motives matter.

◆

Ever do a "motives" check? Truth is, we often do good things with bad motives. It's time to check your motivation. Why are you doing what you're doing (good or bad)? Be honest! If your motivations are self-focused, it's time for a little self-evaluation.

DAY 108

Your sins won't keep Him from hanging out with you.

◆

Ever do something so bad that people didn't want to be around you? There's good news today: God won't ever abandon you, even when you mess up in a huge way. He will stick around, even when others don't.

DAY 109

Choose your attitude!

◆

The remarkable thing is we have a
choice every day regarding the attitude
we will embrace for that day. . . . I am
convinced that life is 10 percent what
happens to me and 90 percent how I
react to it. And so it is with you. . .
we are in charge of our attitudes.

CHARLES SWINDOLL

DAY 110

God is never late.

◆

Sometimes it seems like we serve an
eleventh-hour God. He waits to come
through till the very last minute.
Truth is, it just seems that way.
God's timing is always perfect,
and He's never, never late.

DAY 111

Prosperity isn't just about money.

When you hear the word *prosperity*, you likely think of money. There are many other ways to prosper, however. Our souls can prosper. Our health. Our relationships. Our careers. Anything that we place in God's hands will thrive (or prosper).

DAY 112

God's way is the high way.

◆

It's not always easy to take the high road, is it? This is especially true if we've been falsely accused or wounded in some sort of way. Still, God's way is the high way, so step up! Do the right thing. . . even in hard circumstances.

DAY 113

You really can view life from the sunny side.

◆

Perspective is everything!
Some people see the glass half full;
others, half empty. Some wear a smile,
even when they're going through a
storm; others brood when the skies
are sunny. Today, God wants you to
know that viewing life from the sunny
side will keep your heart lifted.

DAY 114

You can do more than you think.

◆

You gain strength, courage,
and confidence by every experience
in which you really stop to look fear in
the face. You must do the thing which
you think you cannot do.

ELEANOR ROOSEVELT

DAY 115

He sees your tears. . . and He cares.

◆

We go through a lot of valleys, don't we? And sometimes it feels like we're all alone in our pain. The tears flow, but no one seems to notice. Oh, but Someone does notice! God sees those tears. . .and He cares. In fact, His heart breaks alongside yours. Today, He longs for you to know you're not alone in the valley.

DAY 116

Failure is an event, not a person.

◆

Have you ever called yourself a failure? Perhaps someone else put that label on you. Here's the truth: People aren't failures. Failure is an event—something that happens. It's not a person. No matter how many times you mess up, you will never be a failure.

DAY 117

You should be on the lookout for serendipitous moments.

◆

Serendipitous moments happen all the time. We "just happen" to run into someone, then end up falling in love. We "just happen" to get a check in the mail on the very day we were praying for a financial miracle. God loves to surprise us with those serendipitous moments!

DAY 118

Tomorrow, today will be behind you.

◆

Having a bad day? Ready to get
it behind you? It will be gone sooner
than you think. Tomorrow,
today will be nothing more than
a hazy yesterday.

DAY 119

Input and output aren't just computer terms.

We are products of our environment, whether we want to admit it or not. What we put in eventually comes out. That's why it's so important to "input" good things (good attitudes, good words, good thoughts) because they will surely come out for all to see!

DAY 120

The hard stuff is made harder when you add anxiety.

◆

Life is hard enough without adding stress. Oh, we don't mean to. We don't set out to let anxiety rule the day. But one thing leads to another and before long we're unraveling at the seams. Today, make up your mind not to add stress to whatever problems you're facing.

DAY 121

Life is full of new beginnings.

◆

Fresh starts! New beginnings!
Oh, how wonderful they are.
If you feel like you've been stuck. . .
like beginning again is impossible,
there's good news today! You have
the opportunity to start fresh.

DAY 122

You are more valuable to God than all of creation.

◆

Think about it! The sun, the moon, the stars. . .snow-capped mountains, a field of flowers, a majestic ocean. In God's eyes, you are far more valuable than all of them put together!

DAY 123

You can keep running, even when you can't see the finish line.

Ever feel like you're running a marathon? The finish line is so far off in the distance that you can't even see it? That's part of the journey. . . trusting God to guide you until the finish line is in sight. So, keep running!

DAY 124

Courage and wisdom walk hand in hand.

◆

Courage is what it takes to stand up
and speak; courage is also what it takes
to sit down and listen.

WINSTON CHURCHILL

DAY 125

Greater things are coming.

Many people believe their best days are behind them. Today, the Lord wants you to know that He's got great plans for you. No matter how great yesterday was, tomorrow can be even better.

DAY 126

The tasks He puts in front of you are doable.

◆

Have you ever been given an
assignment that felt impossible?
Maybe you're facing one now.
Here's the good news: God won't
put anything in your path unless He's
confident it's doable. Lean on Him.
Together, you will get the job done.

DAY 127

Your soul can be satisfied in Him.

◆

We tend to get dissatisfied easily,
don't we? We're easily bored.
Our expectations are unrealistic.
Today, God wants you to know that
true satisfaction really is possible—
your soul (heart, mind) can be
satisfied in Him.

DAY 128

Faster is not always better.

◆

Maybe you're one of those people who tears through a project, moving as fast as you can. Remember, faster isn't always better. Slow and steady wins the race!

DAY 129

Knock and the door will be opened.

◆

Ever feel like doors are being slammed
in your face? You don't have to live
that way. Matthew 7:7 (NIV) says:
" 'Ask and it will be given to you;
seek and you will find; knock and
the door will be opened to you.' "
Today, keep knocking.

DAY 130

You have a Shepherd who cares for you.

◆

Ever feel like a little lost sheep? Wondering if the big, bad wolf is out to get you? Take heart! You have a Shepherd who cares for you and is watching over you to protect you.

DAY 131

You can be excited about each new day!

◆

Ever get that ho-hum feeling? Life just doesn't seem to have the same pizzazz it used to have? Today, God wants you to know that He can invigorate you for the journey ahead. You really can get excited about each new day!

DAY 132

Giving yourself away is the best way to find yourself.

◆

Wondering how to find yourself?
The very best way is to give yourself
away. Care for the needs of others.
Give of yourself. Feed the homeless.
Share a meal with an elderly person.
In doing so, you will
surely find yourself.

DAY 133

Being rich and famous isn't the answer.

◆

I think everybody should get rich and famous and do everything they ever dreamed of so they can see that it's not the answer.

JIM CARREY

DAY 134

With a teeny-tiny bit of faith you can move mountains.

◆

Is there a mountain in your path?
Something standing between you and
your dream? You don't have to climb
it. You don't have to tunnel through it.
You don't have to trek around it.
You just have to speak to it
"Mountain, get out of my way!"

DAY 135

Nothing is impossible for God.

◆

How often do we use the words, "That's impossible!" To us, many things seem out of the realm of possibility. Sometimes we forget that nothing is impossible for God!

DAY 136

If you're weak and weary, God will give you rest.

◆

Ever been so tired you couldn't sleep?
Rest eluded you? Thank goodness,
these seasons don't go on forever.
Take a deep breath and lean on God,
who longs to give you the rest you need.

DAY 137

You can never out give God.

◆

Do you consider yourself a giver?
You love to help other people out?
Doesn't it feel good to help? If giving
is your passion, then God smiles down
on you. He's the greatest giver in the
world! He gave you life, after all!

DAY 138

You can be a need-meeter.

◆

The place God calls you to is the place where your deep gladness and the world's deep need meet.

Frederick Buechner

DAY 139

You can be as happy as you make up your mind to be.

◆

Don't you just love people with a cheerful attitude? It's almost as if they've made up their minds to be happy, no matter what. Today, the Lord wants you to know that half the battle is in the attitude.

DAY 140

God can give you courage to step out, even when you're afraid.

◆

Some days we don't feel like putting one foot in front of the other. We face challenges so great that we're overwhelmed. When you walk with God, courage comes from a place deep within. He truly gives you the wherewithal for the journey.

DAY 141

Living Forward

◆

Life can only be
understood backwards;
but it must be lived forwards.

SOREN KIERKEGAARD

DAY 142

The victory is yours!

◆

We don't always feel victorious, do we?
Sometimes we let discouragement take
the upper hand. Victorious people
have a different attitude. They feel
victorious even when the battle hasn't
been won yet. They see themselves as
overcomers. What about you?
How do you see yourself?

DAY 143

You were made for relationships.

◆

We were never meant to go it alone.
God created us to be in relationship
with others. Today, spend some time
thanking Him for the relationships
He's placed you in.

DAY 144

Your real treasure isn't at the bank.

◆

If you're like most people, you would love to see your bank account grow over time. It's always a good idea to save up for a rainy day. However, God wants you to know that your real treasure isn't something that can be measured in dollars and cents. Your real treasure is waiting for you. . .in heaven.

DAY 145

You are stronger than you think.

◆

Some days we feel about as strong
as a limp noodle. The energy has
drained out of us. On those days,
we have to rely on God, who is our
ultimate strength. When we do,
we find a renewed "zap" of energy
and wherewithal. It's not a fake energy.
Oh no! This is the real deal!

DAY 146

You can be strengthened by joy.

◆

Did you know that joy is an energizer? It's true! When you choose joy (even in the tough circumstances) you'll find yourself invigorated with new, unexplainable strength!

DAY 147

You're not a survivor. . . you're a thriver!

◆

Today, the Lord wants you to know
that calling yourself a "survivor"
isn't the whole truth. Even if you've
been through some really tough stuff,
you're more than a survivor. . .
you're a thriver!

DAY 148

The future comes one day at a time.

◆

Sometimes we get in a hurry.
We want tomorrow to come. . .today!
Right now! We don't want to wait.
The future is coming, but it's never in
a hurry. It comes one day at a time,
just as it has for thousands of years.

DAY 149

Fresh air and sunshine are good for the soul.

◆

If life is draining you, try stepping outside! There's something rather magical about fresh air and sunshine. The great outdoors can transport you beyond your daily woes to a place where birds are singing, clouds are transformed into characters, and the breeze feels like a heavenly song being played over you.

DAY 150

No one is too great to serve.

◆

Some people come across as high and mighty, don't they? Worse yet, they act like they're too good (or too important) to perform certain menial tasks. Today, God wants you to know that everyone—great and small—is called upon to serve.

DAY 151

You can get mad without sinning.

◆

Did you know that getting angry isn't a sin? It's what you do with that anger that concerns God. If you find yourself angry, take a deep breath. It really is possible to let it go. . . before things get explosive!

DAY 152

Life comes in seasons.

◆

Nothing lasts forever. Think about that. No season—good or bad— lasts beyond its times. If you're facing a difficult challenge today, remember. . .it's just a season. This season will surely pass.

DAY 153

Sail away from the safe harbor.

◆

Twenty years from now you will
be more disappointed by the things
you didn't do than by the ones you
did. So throw off the bowlines, sail
away from the safe harbor. Catch the
trade winds in your sails. Explore.
Dream. Discover.

MARK TWAIN

DAY 154

God cares about what you're going through.

◆

It's easy to imagine you're all alone in the world. . .that no one knows or cares what you're going through. Still, the Bible is clear on this one. God knows everything you're facing, and He cares.

DAY 155

It pleases God to bless you.

◆

If you're a parent, then you know
that wonderful feeling of giving
special gifts to your child. There's
nothing like the look of wonder
in a youngster's eyes on Christmas
morning. Today, God wants you to
know that He is a loving Father,
and He gets great pleasure out of
blessing His kids, too.

DAY 156

When you are weak, He is strong.

◆

Did you know it's okay to admit you're weak? There are truly times when it's better to say, "I can't handle this! I'm worn out!" than to pretend we're okay. In those times, we must rely on God, who longs to strengthen us from the inside out.

DAY 157

Pride can act like a poison.

◆

Ever met someone who sounded
(and felt) like poison?
Pride (arrogance) can puff you up
with a venom that affects everyone
who comes in contact with you.
Today, spend some time willfully
letting go of all pride.

DAY 158

We can celebrate our unique gifts.

◆

Ever feel like you're different from other people? The things that interest them don't interest you? Their talents and abilities are completely different from your own? Instead of trying to be like them, celebrate your unique talents and interests.

DAY 159

God speaks through His Word.

◆

How many times have you said,
"I wish God would just show me what
to do!" or "Why doesn't He just speak
to me?" Truth is, He speaks to you
every time you open the Bible.
His Word is loaded with
instructions for everyday living.

DAY 160

God has unlimited anytime minutes.

◆

Ever been in the middle of a call with someone who said, "I'd better hang up now. I'm almost out of minutes." Here's the good news: God is never out of minutes. He can chat with you 24/7 and you'll never hear the words, "Oops, I've got to go now!"

DAY 161

Optimism is essential to success.

◆

Optimism is essential to achievement
and it is also the foundation of
courage and true progress.

Nicholas Murray Butler

DAY 162

The truth will set you free.

◆

Sometimes the truth is hard to hear.
It's painful. Still, difficult truth is
always better than a lie. Today,
make up your mind to tell the truth
and to receive the truth.

DAY 163

Holding your tongue is often good advice.

◆

Oh, how we want to tell people
off when they hurt us! They bark and
we bark back. They sting with words,
and we join in the game, adding insult
to injury. Only one problem. . .
we're creating an ever-growing fire.
Biting your tongue is tough,
but in the long run you will save
yourself a lot of grief.

DAY 164

He's standing at the door knocking.

◆

Life can get crazy. . .and loud!
Sometimes we miss things because
the noise level is so high: phone calls,
a knock on the door, text messages.
Today, God wants you to know that
He's standing at the door of your
heart, knocking. Can you hear Him?
He wants to come in and
spend time with you.

DAY 165

It's okay to be yourself.

◆

We live in a day of copycats.
Everyone wants the same phone,
the same car, the same television,
the same Blu-Ray player, the same
gaming system, the same clothing
styles, the same type of house.
Instead of fighting to be like
everyone else, just relax. Be yourself.
There's truly no better person
you could be.

DAY 166

You can be a fruit-bearer.

◆

Some days we're more productive than others. We drop into bed at the end of the night feeling satisfied that we've put in a good day's work. However, even on the days when we're not physically able to keep up, we can still be productive by bearing fruit. What fruit, you ask? Love, joy, peace, patience. . . You get the idea!

DAY 167

Your circle of friends doesn't define you.

◆

Think back to your junior high days. Remember how you wanted to fit into a certain group of friends? Oh, if only you were cool enough to hang out with them! Today, God wants you to know that who you know—who you hang out with—doesn't define you. It's who you are when you're all alone that matters.

DAY 168

To err is human;
to forgive. . .divine!

◆

We all make mistakes. Some seem
bigger than others (and some affect
more lives). We want people to
overlook our mistakes but don't always
repay the favor. We hold grudges.
We refuse to forgive. God's message
of the day is this: Forgive. Let it go.
This is your day to move forward.

DAY 169

Actions really do speak louder than words.

◆

What we say and what we do have to match. We can't say we're going to do something and then walk away and forget about it. God wants us to be people of integrity—people who do what they say, and people who are who they claim to be.

Sticks and stones will break your bones, but words can break your heart.

◆

Remember that old saying, "Sticks and stones may break my bones, but words will never hurt me"? It's not true. Words can cause deep, lifelong wounds. Today, God longs for you to guard your words. Don't wound.

DAY 171

You are powerful in Him.

◆

If you've ever worked out at a gym,
then you know what it's like to be
aware of your strength. The more you
work out, the greater the muscle mass,
the more you can lift. Progress comes
over time. The same is true of our
relationship with the Lord.
The more time we spend with Him,
the stronger we get!

DAY 172

We fight best on our knees.

◆

Some people fight it out in a courtroom. Others duke it out in a boxing ring. Some quarrel with words, sending e-mails back and forth across the Web. Today, God wants you to know that the greatest way to fight is on your knees. . .in prayer.

DAY 173

You don't have to give in to temptation.

◆

Too often we give in to the temptation to eat the wrong thing, say the wrong thing, do the wrong thing. . .without even fighting. You don't have to give in. Look that temptation in the eye and just say no!

DAY 174

The Lord wants you to be His hands and feet.

◆

Ever feel like you need to be doing something for the Lord? Maybe you're so overwhelmed at all of the good things He's poured out on you that you want to give back. You can! With your hands, reach out to people in need. With your feet, walk toward the needy.

DAY 175

You were made for good works.

◆

The Bible is clear that we don't win special favors with God by behaving. However, He did create us to do good things. We don't do them to win brownie points or to earn a bigger eternal score. We do them because we're created in the image of God, the greatest good deed doer of all time!

DAY 176

God will lift you out of the pit.

◆

Ever feel like you've fallen to the bottom of a deep pit? Like you're surrounded by darkness? Like there's no way out? Today, from the depth of your soul, cry out to God. His greatest desire is to lift you from that pit.

DAY 177

He is worthy of all your praise.

◆

We are often painfully aware of our unworthiness. We mess up, then slink away into the shadows, feeling like the scum of the earth. Even when we're in our lowest state, God is still worthy of our praise. He's not waiting until you get your act together; He wants to meet you today.

DAY 178

The only way to be filled is to empty yourself.

◆

Do you ever cry out, "I just feel so empty inside!" If so, then you're in the perfect place for God to fill you up—with His joy, His laughter, His courage.

DAY 179

Soul food is always on the menu.

◆

Before we can take care of others,
we've got to take care of ourselves.
This is especially true of our heart,
mind, and soul. Feed yourself daily
from the Word of God to
satisfy your soul.

DAY 180

It's better to offer love than criticism.

◆

We have a tendency to offer critique, even when the person we're critiquing doesn't expect it. Next time you feel that nudge, try offering words of love instead.

DAY 181

He's still a miracle-working God.

◆

Some are of the mindset that God is no longer in the miracle-working business. . .that all miracles ceased with the death of the last apostle. It's not true! Today, God wants you to know that He's still in the miracle-working business!

DAY 182

His strength is made perfect in your weakness.

◆

When we are at our weakest, God is
at His strongest. So, don't be afraid to
admit your weakness! It is in that very
moment that God's strength is made
perfect inside of you.

DAY 183

A bend in the road is not the end of the road.

◆

Oh, how we wish we could see all the way down the road. Fears kick in when we can't see around the bend. We imagine the worst. Today, God wants you to know that the bend in the road doesn't have to be a fearful place. It's not the end of the road; it's just a place where you can learn to trust Him more.

DAY 184

Managing your time well is essential to success.

◆

The ability to concentrate and to use
your time well is everything if you
want to succeed in business—or in
anything else, for that matter.

LEE IACOCCA

DAY 185

You can call on Him 24/7.

◆

Have you ever arrived at a store just as it was closing up for the day? If so, then you know the disappointment of "almost" making it. You'll never have an "almost" encounter with God. No matter when you call on Him, He will be there.

You don't have to work to earn His love.

◆

Remember when you were a kid and
your parents kept a "chore chart"
on the wall? You got a check mark
for making your bed, another check
mark for keeping your room clean,
and another for folding your clothes.
Thank goodness God doesn't work
off of the same system. Even if there
are no "checks" on your chart,
He loves you just the same!

DAY 187

God will set your feet upon a rock.

◆

Ever feel like you're slip-sliding along?
Like you're wading in quicksand?
Today, God wants you to know that
He can set your feet on a rock
(a solid place).

DAY 188

You have a shelter from life's storms.

◆

Where do you run when it's storming?
To the nearest shelter of course!
Life presents us with many storms,
and we run to all sorts of crazy places
trying to find shelter. There's only one
place that makes sense, however.
Run straight to the Lord.
He's the ultimate storm shelter!

DAY 189

He longs to spend time with you.

◆

If you've ever been in love, then you know what it feels like to yearn for someone. To pine for them. To count the hours until you see them again. Did you know that God is pining for you right now? It's true. He loves you that much!

DAY 190

Opportunities can be grown into something great.

◆

We're given hundreds of opportunities
each year. Some make more sense
than others. Today, God wants you to
know that many of the opportunities
He sends your way are going to grow
(morph) into something far beyond
what you ever expected.
Prepare yourself for big things.

DAY 191

The Bible is your road map.

◆

Are you navigationally challenged?
Don't know north from south,
east from west? Wish there was some
sort of spiritual GPS to guide you?
Good news. . .there is! God's Word is
the best navigational tool you could
ever use. It guides you straight
into His arms.

DAY 192

Childlike faith
is a good thing.

◆

Isn't it wonderful to watch a small child leap into your arms? He's sure you'll catch him. No doubt about it, God wants us to approach Him with the same childlike faith—sure that He will not only catch us but lift us above our circumstances.

DAY 193

The opinions of others shouldn't bother you.

◆

Are you a people pleaser? Do you
worry too much about what others
think? Today, God wants you to know
that only one opinion matters—His.

DAY 194

You can be a voice for truth.

◆

Who stands up for those who can't take a stand themselves? You can! That's right. . .you! Today, make up your mind to be a voice for truth. No, it isn't always popular. But you can rest your head on the pillow at night knowing you've made a difference in the world.

DAY 195

You've got to face the cloud to find the silver lining.

◆

Likely you've heard the old expression,
"Every cloud has a silver lining."
It's true. But it's time to face facts:
You won't see the silver lining if you
don't face the clouds. Stormy seasons
will come. Don't run from them.
If you look beyond the clouds,
you'll see that shimmering lining.

DAY 196

You don't have to claw your way to the top.

◆

These days folks scratch and claw their way up the corporate ladder, not really paying much attention to who they step on along the way. God wants you to know that He's in the "elevating" business. No need to step on anyone along the way. He will promote you when the time is right.

DAY 197

You don't have to see yourself as a victim anymore.

Maybe you've been through some terrible experiences. You were abused as a child or badly wronged on the job. Here's the good news: that event does not define you. It's time to let go of the "victim" label. It's no longer yours because you've been set free.

DAY 198

You can overcome a hot temper.

◆

Oy, that temper! It's like a pot of stew, simmering on the stove. Any moment now, it could boil over! God wants you to grab hold of your temper, give it a firm shake, then send it packing. A calm, cool answer will go a lot further toward healing a relationship than an overspill!

DAY 199

It's okay to admit when you're struggling.

◆

So many of us pretend we're okay
when we're really not. We put on
a front, acting like we've got it all
together. It would be better to open
up and admit you're struggling.
That way you're being completely
honest and others will
respond to your need.

DAY 200

What you do is not as important as who you are.

◆

We put such stock in what we do,
don't we? We brag about our careers,
our aspirations, our over-the-top plans
to make something of ourselves.
Today, God wants you to know that
what you do is good, but who you are
is better. Be someone you can
be proud of.

DAY 201

Your life is a gift to God.

◆

What we are is God's gift to us.
What we become is our gift to God.

ELEANOR POWELL

DAY 202

Taking a Sabbath rest is a good thing.

◆

Ah, sweet rest! After a long week,
you're overdue for a break!
God knows this and even set aside
a special day just so you can kick your
feet up and clear your head. Make sure
you celebrate the Sabbath by kicking
back and resting!

DAY 203

God answers knee-mail.

◆

We send all sorts of mail these days—
snail mail, e-mail, and even overnight
mail. If you're looking for a sure
answer, however, the best kind of
mail you can send is knee-mail.
Spend some time in prayer and
you will surely get your answer.

DAY 204

The light at the end of the tunnel is not a train.

◆

Have you ever felt like you were
nearing the end of a chaotic period?
Like you could finally see the light in
the distance? Here's some good news:
That light is not a train. It's a light that
will guide you toward peace
and fulfillment.

DAY 205

Don't fear the opinions of others.

◆

The moment we begin to fear the
opinions of others and hesitate to
tell the truth that is in us, and from
motives of policy are silent when we
should speak, the divine floods
of light and life no longer
flow into our souls.

ELIZABETH CADY STANTON

DAY 206

God is still in the healing business.

◆

It's true! God is the same—yesterday, today, and forever. If He did it for the mighty men and women in Bible days, He will do it for you. Today, you can believe God to heal you— heart, soul, and body.

DAY 207

You are going to make mistakes.

◆

You're not perfect. Face it. Like everyone else on the planet, you're going to make mistakes. Problem is, most people don't like to acknowledge their mistakes. Give yourself permission to mess up. Admit your flaws. There! Doesn't that feel good?

DAY 208

All things work together for good.

◆

Sometimes it's hard to imagine that
God could work all things together for
good. After all, some of the things we
go through are pretty awful. Some day
we'll have the benefit of hindsight and
will be able to see more clearly just
how the Lord pieced all of our life
experiences—good and bad—
into one large, beautiful quilt.

DAY 209

Pacing yourself
is a good idea.

◆

Go, go, go! What image does that
sentence conjure up? Images of
someone racing toward the goal, right?
Today, the Lord wants you to know
that pacing yourself is a better way to
reach your goal. One foot at a time.
One step at a time. Steady, she goes!

DAY 210

Life in the spotlight isn't all it's cracked up to be.

◆

Some people dream of making it big, of seeing their name up in lights. Unfortunately, life in the spotlight isn't always as thrilling as you might imagine. Today, make up your mind to step away from that tempting light.

DAY 211

God doesn't make mistakes.

◆

If someone asked you to list all of the mistakes you'd ever made, how much paper would it take? A lot, right? If we gave the Lord that same assignment, He wouldn't need any paper at all. Why? Because He's never made a mistake. When He created you, He knew exactly what He was doing!

DAY 212

God can turn lemons into lemonade.

◆

Likely you've heard the old expression
about turning lemons into lemonade.
Some problems are so big, however,
that it's hard to imagine turning
them into something sweet.
Thank goodness the Lord specializes
in the impossible. He can turn even
the roughest situation around.

DAY 213

God is in the life-changing business.

◆

Don't you love to see things renovated? Rooms, cars, people. . . it's so much fun to watch the transformation! Did you know that God is in the transforming business? Today, He longs to change your life for the better.

DAY 214

Most of the things we worry about are non-eternal.

◆

Have you ever considered the fact that most of the things you worry about won't matter when you're in heaven? It's true! The daily trials and tribulations we go through in this life will soon be behind us. Eternity is forever. Problems are just for a season.

DAY 215

God wants to renew your strength.

Ever wished for a supernatural zap
of strength? A burst of energy?
Sometimes we're too weary to drum
up the physical or emotional strength
to keep going. Thank goodness God
is standing nearby, ready to renew our
strength when we need it most.

DAY 216

You can hold on a little while longer.

◆

Ever feel like you're hanging from a cliff, your fingertips about to lose their grip? Today, God wants you to know that you can hang on awhile longer. He's right there, holding your hands steady.

DAY 217

You can't outrun God.

Many of us spend our lives running
from things—obligations,
relationships, even God. There are
many things you can outrun, but no
matter how fast you are, you can never
outrun God. Today, why not turn and
run toward Him, instead of away?

DAY 218

The clock is not your taskmaster.

◆

Oh, how we let the clock rule us!
It dictates our comings and goings,
and even our mood, at times. It's time
to say good-bye to that non-caring
taskmaster! You can still keep up with
appointments and plans, but they
don't have to rule over you.

DAY 219

There's no business like prayer business.

We spend a lot of time thinking
about our businesses—outside the
home and in—but we don't often
think of prayer as a "business."
It is! In fact, it should be our primary
business! Today, before you head off
to work. . .get down to business!

DAY 220

Fitting in isn't all it's cracked up to be.

◆

Many of us have been trying to "fit in" since childhood. Here's a great secret, one that would've been great to know in junior high: There's a huge difference between finding your fit and fitting in. Finding your fit is critical. Fitting in? Not so much.

DAY 221

You can turn your worries over to God!

◆

Every evening I turn my worries
over to God. He's going to be
up all night anyway.

MARY C. CROWLEY

DAY 222

It's possible to praise. . . even in the storm.

◆

If you've been through a storm
season, you know there is life on the
other side of it. However, there's
also life in the very midst of it.
Even in the middle of the storm—
when things are whirling around
you—you can praise the Lord.

DAY 223

You don't need to worry about tomorrow.

◆

When you hear the word tomorrow, what comes to mind? Are you unnerved, wondering what the future holds? Many people fear the unknown, wondering if it will be kind. Today, God wants you to know that you don't need to worry about tomorrow. He's going to be there with you.

DAY 224

It's okay to fail forward.

◆

If you've tried something but failed, take heart! As long as you're failing in the right direction (forward) progress is being made. Don't let one failure stop you from trying again.

DAY 225

God is doing a new thing.

◆

Ever feel like your life is mundane?
Each day is just the same old, same
old? Well, there's good news today!
Isaiah 43:19 tells us that God is
doing a new thing! He stands by,
ready to spring you into a world
of new possibilities.

DAY 226

We are created in the image of a creative God.

◆

Isn't it fun to think about what God was doing as He created the heavens and the earth? It's just as fun to think about the fact that we're created in His image. That means we're created to be creative, too!

DAY 227

God is your source.

If you've been relying on yourself
to meet your needs (financial or
otherwise), it's time for a reality
check. You are not your source.
No matter how great your job,
how high your income, you're not the
one responsible. God is your source
and He's got you covered!

DAY 228

You can hear a lot in the silence.

◆

What a loud and crazy world we live in. Televisions blare, horns honk, people chatter, children argue, bosses lose their temper. We're surrounded on every side. That's why it's important to step away from the noise as often as we can. You can hear a lot in the silence.

DAY 229

There is no fear in love.

◆

With love comes trust. With trust,
fear vanishes. That's one reason it's
so important to know that God loves
you. You can trust His love. Resting in
it means you have nothing to fear.

DAY 230

You can stand on God's promises.

◆

If God said something, He will do it.
His promises are rock-solid. So solid,
in fact, that you can stand on them.
They're not going anywhere!

DAY 231

Character matters.

A good character is the best
tombstone. Those who loved you
and were helped by you will remember
you when forget-me-nots have
withered. Carve your name on hearts,
not on marble.

CHARLES H. SPURGEON

DAY 232

You can battle giants and win.

◆

Up against a huge giant? Feel like you're small in comparison? There's good news! Like David facing the mighty Goliath, you can face your giants and win. With God's help, there will be victory!

DAY 233

Things will get better.

◆

Ever feel like you're on a downhill slide? Like things are progressively getting worse? Today, God wants you to know one thing: it will get better. No matter how tough things have been, your tomorrows are going to be better than your yesterdays.

DAY 234

Prodigals are welcomed back home.

◆

If you've ever welcomed a prodigal child back into your home then you know the joy of reuniting with someone you thought you'd lost. In that same way, God welcomes us back when we've strayed. Why not run into His arms today?

DAY 235

Beauty is more than skin deep.

◆

Some people are undeniably beautiful. They possess the faces and bodies you see on magazine covers. There's good news today! Even if you weren't blessed with physical beauty, you can radiate great beauty by letting your spirit shine. Beauty is definitely more than skin deep!

DAY 236

God has big plans for you!

◆

God's plans for us are bigger than we can imagine! Jeremiah 29:11 (NIV) says, "For I know the plans I have for you," declares the LORD, "plans to prosper you and not to harm you, plans to give you hope and a future." What an exciting future you have!

If a million people say a foolish thing, it's still a foolish thing.

◆

Sometimes we spend so much time listening to so-called experts that we don't realize when they're wrong. Today, instead of being duped, ask for the Lord's opinion. He will never give you foolish advice.

DAY 238

You might go through high waters, but you will not drown.

◆

Ever feel like you need a life preserver to get through the high waters of life? It's true. . .we go through some deep places. How wonderful to know that the Lord is holding us up. The waters might rage around us, but we're not going down!

DAY 239

God would rather be your pilot than your co-pilot.

◆

Handing over the controls of your life to the Lord might sound impossible, but He's got the flight plan memorized! He's also skilled at life-flights. You can trust Him!

DAY 240

God gave you a sound mind.

◆

Ever feel like your thoughts are cloudy? Like things don't make sense? Shake off those feelings. Don't give in to them. Remember the words of Isaiah 26:3 (NIV): "[God] will keep in perfect peace those whose minds are steadfast, because they trust in you."

DAY 241

You can forgive, even when you can't forget.

Sometimes we're so deeply wounded
that it leaves a lasting scar. Did you
know it's possible to forgive, even
when the scars are visible? You might
not forget, but forgiveness is a choice
you can make. A tough choice, sure. . .
but the right one.

DAY 242

If we worry about tomorrow, we will miss today.

◆

Sometimes we're so busy fretting over
the unknown (tomorrow and beyond)
that we miss the obvious: today!
Take a deep breath. Look around you.
Today is happening!
Don't let it pass you by.

DAY 243

Your children are your legacy.

◆

Have you ever thought about what you will leave behind when you're gone? Many focus on leaving things like money, jewels, or houses. If you're a parent, the greatest gift you will leave the world is your children. They are your legacy, your inheritance.

DAY 244

It's okay to dream big.

◆

Have you ever been accused of being
a dreamer? Maybe some people think
your goals or plans are unrealistic.
Don't let that stop you! Today, God
wants you to know that
dreaming big is okay.

DAY 245

God is hopelessly devoted to you.

◆

Have you ever been so in love that you couldn't see straight? If so, then you have some indication of God's love for you. He's moon-eyed over you!

DAY 246

Who you are is not who you're going to be.

◆

Today, God wants you to know that you don't have to settle for a mundane life. Don't buy the lie that you'll never "be" anything (or anyone) other than who you are today. Sure, there's a gap between who you are and who you could be. . .but it's a gap you can sail over!

DAY 247

The Bible is more than a history book.

◆

The Bible is filled with amazing
stories from thousands of years ago,
but it's so much more than a history
book. Each story is true, and contains
relevant, practical information to
help you live your life in the
twenty-first century.

DAY 248

We possess power beyond measure.

◆

Our deepest fear is not that we are inadequate. Our deepest fear is that we are powerful beyond measure. . . . You are a child of God. Your playing small doesn't serve the world. There's nothing enlightened about shrinking so that other people won't feel insecure around you. We were born to make manifest the glory of God that is within us.

Nelson Mandela

DAY 249

You don't have to be ashamed of your mistakes.

◆

God never intended us to walk around, overwhelmed by shame. Once we experience His forgiveness, we can lift our eyes and our heads and face today (and tomorrow) with confidence, not held back by the mistakes of our yesterdays.

DAY 250

God has given you power to bring about change!

◆

Ever wish you could make a difference in the world? You can! Your attitude, your willingness to help those in need, your generous nature. . .all of these can play a role in bringing about change in your world. Make up your mind to be a change-maker!

DAY 251

Work is meant to be enjoyed.

◆

Did you know that God never intended for your workday to be mundane or painful? Consider the words of Ecclesiastes 3:22 (NIV): "So I saw that there is nothing better for a person than to enjoy their work, because that is their lot. For who can bring them to see what will happen after them?"

DAY 252

A relaxed state of mind is a healthy state of mind!

◆

We can get so caught up in the anxieties of our work, our families, and our finances that we feel wound up all the time. Today, take a deep breath. Relax. Trust God. Only in that relaxed state can your body regenerate.

DAY 253

You were created in the image of a creative God.

◆

We are creative beings. We're
always thinking of ways to use
our creativity to enrich our lives.
No need to apologize for that!
We're created in the image of
a creative God, after all!

DAY 254

You don't have to figure it all out.

◆

Ever feel like life is one big pop quiz that you're failing? Don't fret! It's not. You don't have to have all of the answers. God is a very forgiving teacher, and He grades on a grace-filled curve.

DAY 255

You have an ever-present help in time of need.

Do you ever wish you could just snap your fingers and a hero would come rushing in to save the day? You can. . . and He will! God is waiting for you to turn to Him with your problems and pain. He is your ever-present help in time of need.

DAY 256

He gives strength to the weak.

◆

Looking for the strength-building technique? The kind that invigorates you, even on the toughest of days? Isaiah 40:29 (NIV) says that "[God] gives strength to the weary and increases the power of the weak." What great news!

DAY 257

Your tomorrow can be better than your yesterday.

◆

Perhaps you've walked through
a tough season in your life. If so,
lift that chin! Look up! Just because
you've been through a difficult time
doesn't mean tomorrow is going to
be difficult. Better days lie ahead.
Face them with hope.

DAY 258

Your perspective
is critical.

◆

You can tell the size of your God
by looking at the size of your worry
list. The longer your list,
the smaller your God.

UNKNOWN

DAY 259

You can be a light in the darkness.

◆

Remember that song we used to sing as kids. . .the one about letting our little light shine? It is possible, even when you feel as if you're surrounded on all sides by darkness, to let your little light shine. You can make a difference in your workplace, your community, your home, and your country.

DAY 260

Every day can
be your best day.

◆

Do you look forward to each new
day with great excitement? You would,
if you realized that every single day of
the week has the potential to be your
best day ever! Make up your mind to
celebrate each day as a victory.

DAY 261

He sings over us.

◆

This is hard to imagine, but God celebrates our existence. It's true. According to Zephaniah 3:17 (NIV), "[He] will rejoice over you with singing." Today, the Lord wants you to imagine Him doing the happy dance overhead while you celebrate His goodness here below.

DAY 262

You can make someone's day special by speaking a kind word.

◆

Isn't it amazing how a kind word—
just a simple compliment or hello—
can make someone's day?
Today, make a point to reach out
to someone with a smile, a cheerful
greeting, or a flattering comment.

DAY 263

Everybody falls sometimes.

◆

Life provides plenty of opportunities to trip and fall, doesn't it! Falling isn't the problem. Staying down is. When you fall—and you will—do your best to bounce back up again. Remember, you're not alone. We all fall. But it takes a resilient person to get back up and begin again.

DAY 264

You are a new creation. The old has passed away.

◆

Have you ever watched a plant— nearly dead—spring back to life again with water and sunshine? If so, then you've witnessed the miracle of rebirth. The plant is like new. Today, God wants you to know that the same rebirth is possible in your life. Allow Him to make you brand new.

DAY 265

His pain is your gain.

◆

If you're an exercise fanatic, then you surely know these words: "No pain, no gain!" It's true, isn't it! However, when it comes to the Lord, He took the pain for you. His pain— the sacrifice of His Son— is definitely your gain!

DAY 266

Expressing your gratitude is a good thing.

◆

The more we express our gratitude
to God for our blessings, the more
He will bring to our mind other
blessings. The more we are aware
of to be grateful for,
the happier we become.

EZRA TAFT BENSON

DAY 267

What you do makes a difference.

Maybe you feel like you're just one teensy-tiny person in a giant world filled with billions of people. You think you can't make a difference. Not true! You were put on this planet to make a difference. Don't ever be convinced otherwise.

DAY 268

Money doesn't have to control you.

◆

What do you think of when you hear the words "the daily grind"? Do you picture yourself slaving away to earn a few bucks to pay the mortgage, light bill, and so on? We need to take a vacation from this sort of thinking. Money is just a means to an end. It's not our boss. We can trust God, even with our finances.

DAY 269

There will be an answer in heaven to the "why" questions.

◆

So many things happen in this life that we don't understand. We can't make sense of them, no matter how hard we try. And asking "why" only gets us more confused. Today, God wants you to know that the "why" questions will be answered in heaven, where there are no more tears and no pain.

DAY 270

There is room in the family for you.

◆

Maybe you grew up in a family where you felt as if you didn't fit in. Perhaps those feelings have spilled over as you've considered joining a local church. Don't be afraid! There's plenty of room in the family for you!

DAY 271

God will make
your path straight.

◆

Ever feel like the road stretched
out in front of you is jagged and
confusing? You're not sure which way
to go? Even if the path appears to be
crooked, God can—and will—
clarify which way to go. Trust Him
each step of the way.

DAY 272

A fool and his money are easily parted.

◆

Spending frivolously is such a temptation, particularly if you're an impulse shopper. After all, you can blow a lot of money in a hurry when you're not paying attention!
This would be a good day to s-l-o-w down. Don't part with that money so quickly. Think it through.

DAY 273

We learn by
trial and error.

◆

We're on a never-ending learning
curve. We make mistakes, correct
them, then try again. Sometimes it
takes several tries to get it right. That's
okay! Just don't give up. Keep on
keepin' on, even if you make a few
mistakes along the way.

DAY 274

Nature sings
God's praises.

◆

If God had wanted to be a big secret,
He would not have created babbling
brooks and whispering pines.

ROBERT BRAUL

DAY 275

Getting in shape can be fun.

◆

Remember when you were a kid in gym class? What fun you had, running laps and doing jumping jacks. Working out is still fun as long as you have a good attitude. Stay in shape, both mentally and physically!

DAY 276

No one else is like you.

◆

Maybe you've heard the old
expression: "When God made you,
He broke the mold!" It's true! You are
unique. You're different. . .and that's
a good thing. Today, God wants you
to celebrate your uniqueness!

DAY 277

If God said it, it's so!

◆

We can't always trust people.
They say they're going to do things. . .
then don't. Today, God wants you
to know that you can trust Him.
If He said it, it's so!

Your security doesn't have to lie in your own accomplishments.

◆

Perhaps you're very accomplished—
a great worker, skilled at what you
do. Even so, your security doesn't lie
in your performance. Even the best
performance doesn't come close to
what God can do through you.

DAY 279

God's timing is perfect.

◆

Sometimes we question God's timing.
We wonder why He waits till the
eleventh hour to work a miracle
and/or pull us through a rough
situation. Here's a newsflash:
God's timing is perfect. He's never late.

DAY 280

God makes Himself known every day.

◆

People see God every day,
they just don't recognize Him.

PEARL BAILEY

DAY 281

Confession really is good for the soul.

◆

It's true! No matter what you've done—good or bad—you'll feel better if you tell someone. Today, if you've been harboring something deep inside of you, open up and share it with someone you can trust.

DAY 282

God has called you by name. You are His!

◆

Remember when you were little and
your mom wanted your attention?
If you came from a large family,
she likely called out the names of your
brothers and sisters before getting
your name right. There's good news
today: God has called you by name!
He doesn't get you mixed up.
You're His precious child!

DAY 283

Life is a great teacher.

◆

If someone asked you to make a list
of all of the lessons you've learned
in your lifetime, could you do it?
Probably not! Life presents us with
an opportunity to learn on a daily—
if not hourly—basis. Life. . .
the best teacher!

DAY 284

Your life can preach a better sermon than any words.

Sometimes our actions don't match the words coming out of our mouth. It's never good to say one thing and do another. People are watching how you live, not so much what you say. Today, make up your mind to preach a great sermon with your life.

DAY 285

God can heal a broken heart.

◆

Imagine a broken glass, shattered into dozens of pieces. Even the best glue in the world couldn't piece it back together. Sometimes our hearts are as broken as that glass. We think that we'll have to live in a state of brokenness. . .forever.
Oh, but it's not true! God is in the heart-mending business!

DAY 286

Your hairs are numbered.

◆

Did you know that God knows how
many hairs are on your head?
It's true! If He knows that much
about you, then surely He cares
about you very much!

DAY 287

It is possible to get rid of a hard heart.

◆

Ever feel like you've been so badly wounded by someone that your heart is hard? Crusty? Unbending? Even if you've felt this way a long time, there's good news today. God knows just how to breathe life into your hard heart, making it soft and pliable once again.

DAY 288

Challenges grow us.

◆

Imagine a little flower, beaten down by the rain. When the sun comes out, however, the flower perks up, energized by the moisture it received during the downpour. Maybe you can relate. Life's challenges (downpours) can make us feel defeated. Thank goodness they're sent to help us grow!

DAY 289

God's ways are higher than our ways.

◆

God is not what you imagine or what you think you understand. If you understand you have failed.

SAINT AUGUSTINE

DAY 290

The more you seek Him, the more you'll find Him.

◆

God is always standing nearby, ready to respond to your call. He's not hiding from you. The more you look for Him (on a daily basis) the more aware you will be of His presence.

DAY 291

Your prayers are powerful.

◆

Remember Popeye? What gave him
the strength he needed to get through
his challenges? Spinach, of course!
Prayer is the "spinach" we need to
pull through life's struggles. It's the
most powerful weapon we have!

DAY 292

It's time to review your purpose in life.

◆

Life without a purpose is a languid, drifting thing; every day we ought to review our purpose, saying to ourselves, "This day let me make a sound beginning."

THOMAS À KEMPIS

DAY 293

One on God's side
is a majority.

◆

If you've ever been ganged up on,
then you know the pressure of
having majority opposition. God
wants you to know that He's on your
side, and with Him, you're always in
the majority!

DAY 294

You don't have to be right all of the time.

◆

Ouch! What? You mean I don't get to
be right all of the time? The answer—
and it's a healthy answer—
is no. You're only right. . .when you're
right. Sometimes (gasp!) we're wrong.
Admitting it is a good thing.

DAY 295

Every ending is a new beginning.

◆

So many times we grieve the ending of something—a job, a school year, a relationship—thinking the best is behind us. Not true! Remember, every ending is a new beginning!

DAY 296

Some questions can't be answered on the Internet.

◆

Some of life's most difficult questions
will never be answered on the
Internet. In fact, some of them won't
even be answered in this lifetime.
We will only know the answer in
heaven. Likely, by then, the answers
to those tough questions won't
matter anymore.

DAY 297

You don't have to let anxiety weigh you down.

◆

Did you know that anxiety is a choice?
It's true! Worry about tomorrow is
never a good idea. It gets you bound
up on the inside. God longs for you
to release that anxiety. Let it go.
There! Doesn't that feel good?

DAY 298

You can be filled with overflowing joy.

◆

Have you ever overfilled a glass with water, tea, or coffee? If so, then you know what the word "overflowing" means. God wants you to be filled with "overflowing" joy today, despite any circumstances you might be walking through.

DAY 299

You can reap what you sow.

◆

It's just common sense. You reap
what you sow. If you sow kindness,
love, and gentleness, you will
(eventually) reap it. If you sow
bitterness, anger, and frustration,
it will swing back around to meet you.
No doubt about it!

DAY 300

The most important things in life aren't things.

◆

How we love our stuff! Cars, the latest
and greatest telephones, computers,
and so on. They're so important to
us. Sometimes our "things" are too
important. We have to remember that
the people God has placed around us
are far more important than anything
we can acquire.

DAY 301

Good deeds offer a great return.

◆

If you've ever invested money, then you know what the words "good return" mean. You invest a certain amount but receive even more as a result. The same is true with good works. When you're good to others, those good deeds come back around to meet you!

DAY 302

God wants to use you in ways you've never even dreamed of.

What if you could see into the future?
You might be stunned to see that God
is going to use you in some miraculous
way to reach out and touch someone
you haven't even met yet. No matter
how big our dreams are, God's dreams
for us are greater still!

DAY 303

The Lord wants to enlarge your vision of who He is.

◆

When I look at the galaxies on
a clear night—when I look at the
incredible brilliance of creation,
and think that this is what God is like,
then instead of feeling intimidated
and diminished by it, I am enlarged. . .
I rejoice that I am a part of it.

MADELEINE L'ENGLE

DAY 304

It's not what you have in your life, it's who you have in your life.

◆

Some people spend their whole lives accumulating stuff—houses, cars, televisions, computers, etc. Today, the Lord wants to remind you that it's about the people, not the stuff.

DAY 305

If you stand for nothing, you'll fall for anything.

◆

Taking a stand for what you believe in takes a lot of fortitude and doesn't always win popularity contests! It's time to stiffen that backbone! Even if it's hard, take a stand.

DAY 306

He is your peace, who has broken down every wall.

◆

Today, God wants to remind you of
the words of Ephesians 2:14 (NIV):
"For he himself is our peace, who
has made the two groups one and has
destroyed the barrier, the dividing wall
of hostility." No more walls!

DAY 307

God's promises shine like stars.

◆

God's promises are like the stars;
the darker the night the
brighter they shine.

DAVID NICHOLAS

DAY 308

He will be a father to the fatherless.

◆

Whether your earthly father played an active role in your life or not, God still longs to prove Himself to be the ultimate Father, one you can trust. Consider the words of Psalm 68:5 (NIV), "A father to the fatherless, a defender of widows, is God in his holy dwelling."

DAY 309

Your story is
going to end well.

◆

Imagine your life story was written
down in a book. Would you wonder
about the yet-unwritten chapters?
This should bring you peace of mind:
You could glance ahead to the ending
and find that everything ends well.
God has you in His care. Your story
is a happily-ever-after one!

DAY 310

God can handle whatever you throw His way.

◆

Those who never rebelled against
God, or at some point in their lives
shaken their fists in the face of heaven,
have never encountered God at all.

CATHERINE MARSHALL

DAY 311

Overlooking an insult shows wisdom.

◆

When we're offended, we often
knee-jerk or return insult for injury.
It takes a lot more wisdom
(and patience) to turn the other cheek.
May this day's reactions be an example
for others and an opportunity
to show great wisdom.

DAY 312

You can listen to life.

◆

The purpose of life is to listen—
to yourself, to your neighbor, to your
world, and to God and, when the time
comes, to respond in as helpful a way
as you can find. . .from within
and without.

FRED ROGERS

DAY 313

You are being molded and shaped into something beautiful.

◆

Ever wish you could predict the future? Wish you could see what sort of person you'll turn out to be? Well, rest easy! God is busy at this very moment, shaping you into something—and someone—of great beauty!

DAY 314

Even when you can't trust people, you can trust God.

◆

People have a tendency to let us down,
don't they? Sometimes betrayal runs
deep. God is good! He's never going
to let you down. You can trust
Him implicitly!

DAY 315

God isn't looking for an advisor.

◆

Most people wish to serve God—
but only in an advisory capacity.

UNKNOWN

DAY 316

To those who believe, all things are possible.

◆

Maybe you're facing something so challenging that fear has you wrapped in its grip. Today, God wants you to trust in the words found in Mark 5:36 (KJV): "Be not afraid, only believe." Lay down that fear. . .and believe.

DAY 317

When you love, you give.

There's something about love that makes us generous. When we love someone, we want the best for them. Sometimes that means reaching deep into our pocketbooks to care for unexpected needs. Sometimes it means giving to the poor or needy. Be prepared! When you love. . .you give.

DAY 318

He will not leave you comfortless.

◆

Have you ever been so emotionally spent that comfort seemed impossible? Even when you're in intense pain, God can—and will—wrap you in His arms. His Spirit breathes new life into your heart, easing the pain and cocooning you in His love.

DAY 319

You were created to make a joyful noise.

◆

Maybe you're not a vocalist.
You can't carry a tune in a bucket.
That shouldn't stop you from
praising God with a song. Follow
the instruction in Psalm 98:4 (NASB):
"Shout joyfully to the LORD, all the
earth; break forth and sing for joy
and sing praises."

DAY 320

He is preparing a place for you.

◆

Did you know that God has a special place in heaven for you? When this life is over, you can walk streets of gold, live in a heavenly mansion, and dance past gates of splendor. How wonderful, to imagine God up in heaven, getting it all ready. . . just for you!

DAY 321

Life is a canvas.

◆

Isn't it fun to think about your life like a large canvas? Already the Master Artist has painted some vibrant colors. The fun part? Imagining what colors are yet to come.

DAY 322

Being forgiven doesn't mean you're perfect.

◆

Some people really struggle with the
need for perfection. Rest easy!
God doesn't expect perfection.
He longs for you to do your best
and to walk in relationship with Him.
But when you mess up—and you
will—He stands nearby,
ready to forgive.

DAY 323

Hanging out with likeminded people is fun!

◆

It's always great to find a group of likeminded people, isn't it? When you hang out with people with similar interests and beliefs, you can relax and be yourself. If you're looking for a safe place to spend time with new friends, check out the churches in your area. They're loaded with awesome people. . .just like you!

DAY 324

You can do something.

◆

I am only one, but still I am one.
I cannot do everything, but still I can
do something; and because I cannot
do everything I will not refuse to do
the something that I can do.

EDWARD EVERETT HALE

DAY 325

You don't need to take yourself so seriously.

◆

Some people are far too concerned about the little details of their life— the tiny mistakes, and so on. It's time to lighten up! Don't take yourself so seriously. Not everything is a huge deal. In fact, most of the things we fret over today will mean nothing tomorrow.

DAY 326

Friendships require cultivation.

◆

A friendship can weather most things
and thrive in thin soil; but it needs
a little mulch of letters and phone
calls and small, silly presents every so
often—just to save it from drying
out completely.

PAM BROWN

DAY 327

You can be a seed planter.

◆

When you influence the lives of those around you, you're leaving behind tiny seeds that will blossom, long after that person moves on. Seeds of hope. Seeds of joy. Seeds of encouragement. Today, plant some lovely seeds in someone you meet.

DAY 328

Risk or rash?

◆

There's a huge difference between taking a risk—stepping out in faith—and acting in a rash manner. Life is filled with risks. Just face them with common sense.

DAY 329

Excellent advice!

◆

It was a high counsel that I once heard
given to a young person, "Always do
what you are afraid to do."

RALPH WALDO EMERSON

DAY 330

The number on the scale does not define you.

◆

We let so many things define us—
our job, our talents, our family,
our peers, our coworkers. . .even our
weight. Whether you're chubby, thin,
tall, short, or in-between, you can't
be ruled by how you look or how
much you weigh.

DAY 331

You can feed your faith and starve your doubts.

◆

Sometimes we get in a rut where our faith is concerned. After all, it's easier to get down about something than to invest the time hoping and believing things will turn around in our favor. Today, God wants you to start feeding your faith. When you do, it will grow, grow, grow!

DAY 332

You can be a witness.

◆

Sometimes being a good witness is as
simple as not giving in to temptation.
Even if others around you are setting
a bad example for their peers—
you can stand out in the crowd by
doing the right thing.

DAY 333

Love makes you beautiful.

◆

Have you ever noticed that people who are physically unattractive appear beautiful when they're in love? There's a beauty that radiates from the inside out. Likewise, even the prettiest person can seem ugly when love is lacking. Which would you rather be— lovely on the inside, or the outside?

DAY 334

When God disciplines us, it's only because He loves us.

◆

Most parents know that discipline
is a natural part of raising children.
We don't discipline out of anger,
but rather to see the child grow and
mature into a responsible adult.
Did you know that God sometimes
disciplines His kids, too? Don't let that
news discourage you though. He's the
most loving parent ever!

DAY 335

God will strengthen you.

◆

God says, "Do not fear, for I am with you; do not be dismayed, for I am your God. I will strengthen you and help you; I will uphold you with my righteous right hand" Isaiah 41:10 (NIV).

DAY 336

God specializes in the impossible.

◆

Doesn't it encourage you to know that
nothing is impossible for God?
If you've ever spoken the words
"It would take a miracle," then take
heart! You happen to know Someone
who's in the miracle-working business.
He delights in the impossible, in fact!

DAY 337

Happily-ever-afters do happen.

◆

Maybe you've been wounded by someone who claimed to care about you. Perhaps your relationship didn't end well. Today, God wants you to know that He's got a real (eternal) happily-ever-after planned out for you. Check it out in the Bible. The Prince really does come on a white horse, after all!

DAY 338

God speaks to us in everyday occurrences.

◆

Every happening, great and small,
is a parable whereby God speaks
to us, and the art of life is to get
the message.

MALCOLM MUGGERIDGE

DAY 339

Taking care of your body is important.

◆

When we come to understand that
our bodies are temples, we realize the
importance of caring for them!
1 Corinthians 6:19–20 (NIV) says,
"Do you not know that your bodies
are temples of the Holy Spirit, who is
in you, whom you have received from
God? You are not your own; you were
bought at a price. Therefore honor
God with your bodies."

DAY 340

God loves
chatting with you.

◆

Do you have a good friend, someone
you love chatting with? God calls you
His friend, and He loves spending
time with you in one-on-one
conversation. Today, stop what you're
doing and settle in for a long chat.

DAY 341

God misses you when you don't spend time with Him.

◆

It's hard to imagine God longing for time with His kids, isn't it? You would think He'd be so busy running the world that He wouldn't notice if we missed a few days of hanging out with Him. He's never too busy to spend time with His kids, so crawl up in His lap today.

DAY 342

Living for today is a great idea.

With the past, I have nothing to do;
nor with the future. I live now.

RALPH WALDO EMERSON

DAY 343

God longs to set the prisoners free.

◆

Ever feel trapped? Feel like something has you imprisoned? There's good news today! No matter what has you bound, God longs to set you free! Give it to Him, and watch those prison doors swing wide open.

DAY 344

Life is an amazing race.

◆

Sometimes life feels like an actual
race, doesn't it? You come charging
out of bed in the morning. You race
to the office, other workers buzzing
by you (some appearing to pass you
by). You arrive home (the finish line)
exhausted. Deep breath, runner.
This life is meant to be enjoyable,
not exhausting!

DAY 345

Availability is better than ability.

◆

Sometimes we limit ourselves because we claim we're lacking in the "ability" department. We feel inadequate. There's good news today! God wants you to know that making yourself available to be used is far more important than your ability!

DAY 346

God can't alter the past.

◆

The past is in the past. Perhaps
you wish you could change it.
Unfortunately—or fortunately—
there's no going back. The past can't
be altered. Instead of focusing on
it, however, it's time to live in today.
Today, you have the opportunity to
do the things you wish you'd done
in the past.

DAY 347

God loves your family.

◆

If you've ever worried about a family
member—maybe someone who's
struggling to get by, or perhaps
one who's made poor decisions—
remember this: God loves your family
even more than you do. He's watching
over them, even now.

DAY 348

Afraid? Do it anyway.

◆

It was a high counsel that I once
heard given to a young person,
"Always do what you are afraid to do."

RALPH WALDO EMERSON

DAY 349

Laughter is a smile with the volume turned up.

◆

Have you ever been around someone who loves to laugh? It's as if they took the smile and amplified it. Today, God wants you to know that you don't have to shy away from laughter. Let 'er rip!

DAY 350

It's possible to stand, even when those around you are falling.

◆

Maybe you're watching your friends
tumble, one after the other.
They're giving in to temptation.
Doing things that could destroy
their lives. Just because they're falling
doesn't mean you have to. Take a
step back if you need to,
but keep on standing.

DAY 351

Apathy is never a good thing.

◆

Science may have found a cure for most evils; but it has found no remedy for the worst of them all—the apathy of human beings.

HELEN KELLER

DAY 352

God is the mender of broken hearts.

◆

So many times in life we end
up broken-hearted. Romantic
relationships end. Friendships are
torn apart. We're hurt—
psychologically or emotionally—
by a boss who is only thinking of the
company. Today, take that broken
heart and give it to the Lord,
who longs to mend it with His love.

DAY 353

He's watching over His Word to perform it.

◆

Ever wondered if God is going to do what He promised in the Bible He would do? He answers that question Himself in Jeremiah 1:12 (NASB) when He said: "I am watching over My word to perform it."

DAY 354

You shouldn't borrow sorrow from tomorrow.

◆

Maybe you're facing something really sad—a friend is dying, your finances are dwindling, your job situation appears to be ending. Instead of focusing on the potential sadness of tomorrow, hang tight to today. There are great blessings in the here and now. Don't miss them!

DAY 355

Hope is a precious commodity.

◆

Ever wish you had a hidden stash of gold or silver? Both metals are precious and worth a lot of money. Did you ever think about the fact that hope is precious, too? In some ways, it's more valuable than gold or silver, because it has the capability of energizing you for the tasks ahead.

DAY 356

You are an inventor!

◆

We are all inventors, each sailing out
on a voyage of discovery, guided each
by a private chart, of which there is no
duplicate. The world is all gates,
all opportunities.

RALPH WALDO EMERSON

DAY 357

Debt-free living is a good thing.

◆

It's easy to get trapped into thinking we deserve the best of everything. . . and we deserve it now! A bigger house, a more expensive car— we're willing to mortgage ourselves to the hilt to have what we want. Today, God wants you to know that He longs to loose you from the chains of debt.

DAY 358

If God is for us, who can stand against us?

◆

Ever feel outnumbered? Like you're surrounded on all sides? You are never alone, even in the middle of the battle. With God on your side, thousands could stand against you, but they would all come out losers in the end.

DAY 359

God longs to put the broken pieces together.

◆

Man is born broken. He lives by mending. The grace of God is glue.

EUGENE O'NEIL

DAY 360

If you aim at nothing, you will surely hit it.

◆

Imagine you went to the shooting range to practice, only to discover all of the targets had been removed. You would have nothing to aim at. How often do we go through life with no aim? We wander with no sense of direction, then wonder why we feel lost. Today, set your aim! Find the target. Then, go for it!

DAY 361

You really can do the thing you're afraid of.

◆

Ever been challenged to do
something difficult? Something that
really frightened you? Maybe you
stopped just shy of doing it.
Fear wrapped you in its tentacles.
Today, God wants you to know that,
with His help, you really can do the
very thing you're afraid to do.

DAY 362

We serve a merciful God.

◆

If you feel like you've really messed up—
like you can't possibly hang out with God
because of something you've done—
think again! Psalm 103:8 (NIV) shows us
that, "The LORD is compassionate and
gracious, slow to anger, abounding in
love." What great news!

DAY 363

Give and take:
it's all in the attitude.

◆

Blessed are those who can give
without remembering and take
without forgetting.

ELIZABETH BIBESCO

DAY 364

Opportunities abound.

◆

Each new day presents countless opportunities: to do unto others as you would have them do unto you. To forgive. To praise your way through tough times. To make good choices. Opportunities for goodness abound!

DAY 365

God loves it when you count your blessings.

◆

Count your blessings. Once you realize
how valuable you are and how much
you have going for you, the smiles
will return, the sun will break out, the
music will play, and you will finally
be able to move forward with the life
that God intended for you with grace,
strength, courage, and confidence.

OG MANDINO

Notes

....
....
....
....
....
....
....
....
....
....
....
....
....
....
....
....
....
....
....
....
....
....

Notes

....
....
....
....
....
....
....
....
....
....
....
....
....
....
....
....
....
....
....
....
....
....

Notes

....
....
....
....
....
....
....
....
....
....
....
....
....
....
....
....
....
....
....
....
....
....
....

Notes

. . . .
. . . .
. . . .
. . . .
. . . .
. . . .
. . . .
. . . .
. . . .
. . . .
. . . .
. . . .
. . . .
. . . .
. . . .
. . . .
. . . .
. . . .
. . . .

Notes

....
....
....
....
....
....
....
....
....
....
....
....
....
....
....
....
....
....
....
....
....

Notes

....
....
....
....
....
....
....
....
....
....
....
....
....
....
....
....
....
....
....
....
....
....

Notes

....
....
....
....
....
....
....
....
....
....
....
....
....
....
....
....
....
....
....
....
....
....
....

Notes

Notes

....
....
....
....
....
....
....
....
....
....
....
....
....
....
....
....
....
....
....
....
....
....

Notes

Notes

....
....
....
....
....
....
....
....
....
....
....
....
....
....
....
....
....
....
....
....
....
....
....

Notes

....
....
....
....
....
....
....
....
....
....
....
....
....
....
....
....
....
....
....
....
....
....
....

Notes

....
....
....
....
....
....
....
....
....
....
....
....
....
....
....
....
....
....
....
....
....
....
....

Notes

. . . .
. . . .
. . . .
. . . .
. . . .
. . . .
. . . .
. . . .
. . . .
. . . .
. . . .
. . . .
. . . .
. . . .
. . . .
. . . .
. . . .
. . . .
. . . .
. . . .
. . . .
. . . .